I0041092

# PROFIT
# Playbook for Women
The Ultimate Resource Guide
to Building a Successful Business

Melissa J. Nixon

Copyright © 2018 Melissa J. Nixon

All rights reserved. No part of this book may be reproduced or transmitted in any form or by any means, electronic or mechanical, including photocopying and recording, or by any information storage and retrieval system, without permission in writing from author and publisher.

Printed in the United States of America
2018 First Edition

Subject Index:
Nixon, Melissa J.
Title: Profit Playbook for Women - The Ultimate Resource Guide to Building a Successful Business
1.   Business 2. Finance 3. Leadership 4. Entrepreneur 5. Self Help

ISBN: 978-0-692-19451-5
Library of Congress Control Number:  2018911831
Courageous Life Publishing Huntersville, NC

# DEDICATION

This book is dedicated to my client and friend Natalie,
and to *you*, the highly successful,
super fierce CEO of a wildly profitable business

# TABLE OF CONTENTS

# INTRODUCTION

*"Do the best you can until you know better. And*
*when you know better you do better."*
*- Maya Angelou*

Welcome to the **Profit Playbook for Women!** The ultimate resource to take your business to the next level. This is a total 360 guide that looks at your foundation, your business, your leadership, and your progress. All are equally important and can only excel when they are in sync and operating in excellence.

## Why this book?

Whether you are just starting or have been on your grind for a while, you already know that building a business, is one of the hardest things to do. Yet it can be done with the right mindset and tools/resources. According to the National Association of Women Business Owners (NAWBO), women-owned businesses account for 39% of privately-owned firms - which means there are over 11.6 million women-owned businesses. And only 2% of women-owned businesses break $1 million dollars in revenue.

Moreover, a Forbes article entitled, "16 Surprising Statistics about Small Businesses" states:

- Of the 28 million small businesses, 22 million are self-employed
- 52% of small businesses are home-based
- The average revenue of non-employer businesses (those with no additional payroll or employees) is $44,000

As you can see and have probably experienced, there is a huge need for women to grow successful, sustainable, and profitable companies. This all-inclusive guide is designed to help you do just that.

### Who can benefit from the Profit Playbook?
- Aspiring business owners
- Business owners who desire to grow their businesses and bottom line
- Business owners who are looking to expand or rebrand themselves
- Business owners who feel stuck or need support

### How to use this book?
The great thing about this book is that it's a guide and you can use it fit your specific needs. It is the perfect resource to help you:

- Pause and reflect
- Analyze what is going on in your business
- Make your next courageous move

You can use it independently, with accountability partners, or a mastermind group. It is divided into four sections that each look at your:

- For Her Foundation
- For Her Business
- For Her Leadership
- For Her Progress

Read it from cover-to-cover or only focus on the sections that you need help with. Be sure you complete **Section 1: For Her Foundation** which includes a discussion around your best practices, areas where you require more support and so much more. In addition, also leverage **Section 4: For Her Progress** to help measure your results and reflect on what's working and what's not.

**Use with accountability partners or a mastermind group:**
You and your group can leverage the book one of two ways, decide whether:

1. You are going to complete the workbook cover to cover - best designed for long-term groups and programs
2. Or select sections of the workbook to work through and discuss based on your business goals and needs.

Whether you are working through the entire book or leveraging specific areas for certain goals be sure to:

- Answer the questions and do the deeper work in each section
- Be willing to be challenged and challenge others
- Be willing to listen and receive feedback
- Meet regularly with your group
- Set deadlines not only for the exercises in the workbook but also for the actual work you need to *do* in your business

Your next level is just around the corner. Get ready to make your next courageous move.

Your Business Coach & Strategic Thought Partner,

melissa *J. Nixon*

For Her
Foundation

# 1 WHAT'S YOUR WHY?

*"People don't buy what you do, they buy why you do it."- Simon Sinek*

Passion for what you do is great! However, understanding what truly drives what you do and *why* you do it will be the determining factors in the longevity of your business. Many people are great at starting, yet not many are willing to do what it takes to finish strong. As you continue to grow, there will be several obstacles to overcome. The difference between those who give up and those who keep going, is understanding their *WHY?*

Payal Kadakia Pujji, Founder and Executive Chairman of ClassPass, a monthly fitness membership program, had one reason why she started the now half billion-dollar company. She had to solve her own problem. She was a world-class dancer who became frustrated after spending over an hour searching online for an open ballet class in New York City. After so much difficulty, ClassPass was born to create access for not just dancers, but everyone who enjoys fitness, to easily find fitness classes they love. Her *why* has now helped fitness lovers not just in New York City, but also 49 others cities across the U.S.

Things like your drive, work ethic, consistency and the like are important, but *why* are you in business? What need are you trying to fill that isn't already being filled? What legacy do you want to leave?

**Share your why below for any area that matter to you most.**

Personal:

Family:

Customers:

Community:

Philanthropy:

Other:

# 2 WHAT'S YOUR VISION

*"When I dare to be powerful to use my strength in service of my vision, then it becomes less and less important whether or not I'm afraid." - Audre Lorde*

In addition to your *why*, the other important factor that keeps business owners going is their vision. For black French artist Nicholle Kobi, her vision was to become an artist and make a living using her gift of drawing black women in various settings. But for years she listened to a teacher who told her that it would never happen and she became a banker instead. One day, she found the courage to post one of her pieces on Instagram responding to a gesture to share what she loved to do. From there, people started asking for replicas on mugs, t-shirts, and more. Today, not only does Nicholle have a global art business with a full product line, but she has also partnered with major brands and influencers such as Hallmark and Gabrielle Union to create greeting card series. And here is the best part, as a French native, she never even heard of the Hallmark brand when they called to do business with her. Talk about a dream come true!

What is your vision? Whether you are just starting or you have been in business for some time, what is the vision that is fueling you right now? What are you working towards? When you look ahead to the next 3-5 years, what would you like to have accomplished?

# My Vision

_____

_____

_____

_____

_____

_____

_____

_____

_____

_____

_____

_____

_____

_____

_____

_____

_____

_____

_____

_____

_____

_____

_____

_____

_____

_____

_____

_____

_____

_____

_____

_____

_____

_____

_____

_____

_____

_____

_____

# 3 BEST PRACTICES

*"Real integrity is doing the right thing knowing*
*nobody will know whether you did it or not."*
*- Oprah Winfrey*

Our results in life and business are a reflection of who we are and what we do consistently. When you look at your life and business put a checkmark next to each statement that is true.

| My Best Practices: | |
|---|---|
| | I get adequate sleep every night (6 - 8 hours) |
| | I exercise 3 - 5 times a week |
| | I take 1 - 2 vacations a year |
| | I follow a healthy diet |
| | I have boundaries around my work hours |
| | I set weekly goals |
| | I set daily goals |

| | My Best Practices: |
|---|---|
| | I routinely reflect on what I accomplished in my day |
| | I routinely reflect on what I accomplished in my week |
| | I understand the obstacles getting in the way of my business growth |
| | I have no issues asking for help or support from others when I feel overwhelmed |
| | I do periodic research to understand the evolution of trends in my industry and what products or solutions potential clients are looking for |
| | I immediately review my notes from conferences and workshops and create an implementation plan for things most applicable to my leadership and business |
| | I have strategic planning sessions for my business at least once per year |
| | I have and use a business plan to guide my businesses growth |
| | I have and use annual business goals |
| | I have and use a marketing plan |
| | I have and use a PR plan |
| | I have and use a social media strategy |
| | I have and use a sales strategy/plan |
| | I conduct client assessments with past and current clients to understand their biggest problems and what solutions we can provide |
| | I research and implement new marketing strategies to generate more leads instead of depending solely on referrals |

| | My Best Practices: |
|---|---|
| | I am constantly doing things to keep my personal and business brand visible |
| | I invest heavily in our company's marketing |
| | Our company has a client retention strategy |
| | Our company has a client experience plan that it follows from lead generation, client acquisition, to retention |
| | I regularly pause and review my businesses progress as compared to our annual goals monthly |
| | I regularly pause and review my businesses progress as compared to our annual goals quarterly |
| | I have a business coach, mastermind, or accountability partner who regularly stretch and challenge me |
| | I am constantly stretching myself to move out of my comfort zone and play a larger role in my leadership and business |
| | I take full advantage of resource organizations in my area and the opportunities they provide |
| | I regularly review the numbers most important to my business |
| | I invest in my leadership development regularly |
| | I invest in the leadership development of my staff regularly, if applicable |
| | I pray or meditate |

What observations did you notice from completing your best practices?

# 4 COMMON MISTAKES

*"The past is where I learned the lesson. The future is
where I apply the lessons learned."- Unknown*

Without best practices for our self and our business, we are
bound to make the common mistakes that can adversely
impact and even stifle business growth. No one is perfect,
but common mistakes compounded and repeated will most definitely
lead to adverse, long-term and potentially permanent damage. It's not
the small things that can be detrimental to your business; it's the
habitual mistakes you refuse to address. There is a big difference
between you forgot to call someone back yesterday versus not having
a follow-up strategy. These are two totally different circumstances.
Habitual mistakes require work because there must be a behavior
change in what we do, how we think, how we feel, and most
importantly, how we approach business.

I can remember dealing with some counterproductive behaviors
and having an aha moment with a friend not too long after
transitioning from Corporate America to launching my consulting
firm. Transitioning from a 9 - 5 job to full-time entrepreneur was a
big shift. Thankfully I was driven, a self-starter, and passionate. But
the shift between my old role and new role were night and day,
obviously. And there were a lot of things I was going to have to learn
as well as unlearn, like how I planned my weeks. A conversation with
a colleague changed my life. Here I was the visionary excited about

idea after idea but lacked the discipline and organizational skills to implement. I found myself hopping from one idea to the next day after day with too many partially completed projects and tasks to count. That is until my friend Kristi told me how she organizes her week. There were days designated for everything including administrative tasks, business development, personal development, networking and more. Talk about a game-changer. Implementing this system stopped me from creating spiraling behaviors and habits that would adversely impact my business and me.

Listed below are a few common mistakes we make in business. Take a look and check all of the ones that are currently getting in your way. Only check the ones that you have found to be a true stumbling block to the success you know you could have.

- ➤ Lack of self-care
- ➤ Lack of discipline
- ➤ Misuse of time
- ➤ Superwoman syndrome
- ➤ Focus too much on feelings vs facts
- ➤ Lack of planning
- ➤ Lack of capital
- ➤ Lack of a focus
- ➤ Too much busy work
- ➤ Mindset (Insecurity, doubt, self-confidence, courage)
- ➤ Not asking for the sale
- ➤ Not asking your value
- ➤ Lack of collaboration
- ➤ Lack of systems
- ➤ Self-sabotage
- ➤ Comparison
- ➤ Not asking for help
- ➤ Lack of guidance/support
- ➤ Lack of trust in others (i.e. team or colleagues)
- ➤ Lack of follow-up
- ➤ Perfection
- ➤ Other _____
- ➤ Other _____
- ➤ Other _____

Now, here comes the hard part; determining what's *really* getting in your way. Albert Einstein said, "The definition of insanity is doing something over and over again and expecting a different result." This resource will provide you with the right tools and ask you the questions you need to continue to grow the business of your dreams. But it won't matter if there is still one thing getting in your way...YOU!

Since you have identified your best practices and common mistakes, determine "why" you keep making these mistakes?

| Common Mistakes | What's the Real Issue? |
|---|---|
| Lack of consistent follow-up strategy | I am afraid of rejection and that people will say "no". |
| | |
| | |
| | |

How are you going to fix it?

| Common Mistakes | Solution |
|---|---|
| | |
| | |
| | |

# 5 WHERE DO I NEED HELP

*"It takes strength and humility to ask for help."*
*- Melissa Nixon*

The answer is not as simple as I need more clients, more revenue, profits, or any other four-word statement. It's deeper than that. Your need for any of the above is a result of a bigger issue that needs to be clearly identified, resolved, and sustained over time.

Your growth solution will always be contingent upon three things:

- Understanding where you need help
- Prioritizing your areas of need (we have more than one, right?)
- Solving the right problem(s)

When you think about your biggest growth opportunities, is your challenge in generating ideas, implementation or sustainability?

_____

Share your growth challenge:

What area(s) of business are you in need of generating more ideas, implementing or sustaining?

    1. _____

    2. _____

    3. _____

What do you think is getting in your way from moving forward in these areas?

Next, is your sales challenge generating leads, converting leads to customers, or retaining customers?

_____

**Share your sales challenge:**

For your sales challenge what do you see as the biggest obstacle(s)?

    1. _____

    _____

    _____

    2. _____

    _____

    _____

3. _____

_____

_____

Based on your current business challenges and your observations from your best practices, what would you say are your top 2 - 3 priorities right now?

1. _____

_____

2. _____

_____

3. _____

_____

Have you actively started working towards those priorities? If so, what is the progress you've made and what are your next steps?

| Priority: | Progress: | Next Steps: |
| --- | --- | --- |
|  |  |  |
|  |  |  |
|  |  |  |

# 6 WHO'S ON YOUR TEAM?

*"If you want to go fast, go alone. If you want to go far, go together." - African Proverb*

Building a successful company that will leave a legacy takes work. It's not done alone or in silos. It requires what I call a "dream team," even if you are solopreneur. The best question you can ask yourself in this area is, "Do I have the team I want and need?" If the answer is "no," you have to consider what you are willing to do to get the right team members.

**Potential Internal Roles Needed:**
Internal roles and needs vary by business type and size. Listed below are some potential roles:

| Role: | Do You Have? Yes/No | Do You Need? Yes/No | Who can you ask for a referral? |
|---|---|---|---|
| Administrative Assistant | | | |
| Business Development | | | |

| | | | |
|---|---|---|---|
| Payroll | | | |
| Graphic/Web Design | | | |
| Marketing | | | |
| Social Media Manager | | | |
| Copywriter | | | |
| Tech Needs | | | |
| HR Needs | | | |
| Other: | | | |
| Other: | | | |
| Other: | | | |

## External Roles Needed:

| Role: | Do you have? Yes/No | Do you need? Yes/No | Who can you ask for a referral? |
|---|---|---|---|
| Attorney | | | |
| CPA | | | |
| Bookkeeper | | | |
| Financial Planner | | | |
| Publicist | | | |
| Insurance Agent | | | |
| Business Coach | | | |

| Other: | | | |
|--------|--|--|--|
| Other: | | | |
| Other: | | | |

Having the right people in the right role is critical. As a small business, you are required to wear multiple hats while your company grows. However, operating like a one-man show or with limited resources should only be done on a temporary basis.

**Here are few questions to get you closer towards the team you want and need:**

Are there things you need to delegate or outsource but haven't? Yes or No.

If yes, what are they?

At times, do you feel overwhelmed or stressed because you are wearing multiple hats?

If yes, what is either taking up too much of your time or causing you additional stress?

Is it something you can outsource to a person, organization, or automation tool?

If yes, when will you do it?

If no, what will you do to focus more on leading the business?

# 7 RESOURCE GUIDE

While every new phase of business brings its own level of growth challenges, there is no reason you have to go through those challenges alone. There are numerous organizations and learning opportunities to provide the support you need at every level. Many have local chapters which offer:

- Counseling
- Certification
- Funding Opportunities & Resources
- Development Programs & Conferences
- Networking Opportunities & Connections

Are you taking full advantage of any of these organizations? Are you leveraging them in combination with how you learn as well as what support you need? For example, conferences are great, inspiring, and full of content, but once you return to your day-to-day, what additional support do you need? Do you need coaching? Accountability? Or perhaps a mastermind group?

**Here are just a few of the resources and organizations to consider:**

Small Business Association
www.sba.gov

SCORE - *Affiliated with the SBA*
www.score.org

## Women's Business Centers - *Affiliated with the SBA*
www.sba.gov/tools/local-assistance/wbc

## National Association of Women Business Owners (NAWBO)
www.nawbo.org

## Women's Business Enterprise National Council (WBENC)
www.wbenc.org

## Minority Supplier Development Council
www.nmsdc.org

## U.S. Bureau of Labor Statistics
www.bls.gov

## Local Community Colleges
Many community colleges offer continuing education classes as well as business development programs for small business owners. Check with your local college to see what may be a good fit for you and your business.

There are many resource organizations that you may be aware of as well that may be industry or geography specific. What resource organizations do you need to take advantage of from the list above or others?

1. _____
2. _____
3. _____
4. _____

The following resources are also pivotal for every business owner and can take the feeling of isolation away as you grow:

- Private Business Coach
- Mastermind Group
- Accountability Partner(s)

- Business Retreats

Choose the one that best fits how you like to learn best. Do you prefer 1:1 or a small group? How does the thought of a weekend intensive or a year-long mastermind group sound? Either way, how you answer these next few questions will help you to see where you need the additional support.

In this past quarter, who have been the people who have been your accountability or thought-partner? Challenged you in your thinking? Stretched you to play bigger?

1. _____

2. _____

3. _____

This guide is designed to assess if you have the right people, processes, and perspective in place for optimal growth. The good thing is it does not matter where you are today. What matters is your tenacity to build what you want for tomorrow.

# Notes & Reflections

# For Her
# Business

Melissa J. Nixon

# 8 BUSINESS STRUCTURE, FUNDING, & PROTECTION

*"There is no royal flower-strewn path to success. And if there is, I have not found it, for if I have accomplished anything in life it is because I have been willing to work hard." – Madam C.J. Walker, America's first black female millionaire*

If you are a new start-up or considering opening another company, you may be wondering what is the best structure for that business. There are numerous factors to take into consideration such the type of company, growth strategy, and more. Even if you have an existing company, you can't assume that you should use the same structure and process for your next venture.

There are plenty of online and in-person resources such as the SBA (Small Business Administration). In addition, to your personal research, this decision should be made in partnership with your CPA and/or business attorney. Either can help you determine which of the following structure is best:

- Sole Proprietor
- Partnership
- Corporation
- S-Corp
- LLC (Limited Liability Company)

Your decision matters for many reasons including:

- How your company wants to grow
- How your financials are handled
- How your company will be viewed and taxed by the IRS

Even if you already made the decision and established your business without consulting expert advice it is not too late. You may find that another business structure is a better fit for your company and change structures at the appropriate time.

## Access to Capital & Funding

Not every business needs access to capital, especially if there is a low entry into the marketplace. However, there are companies who need start-up capital to get going or even capital to keep going.

Many of the organizations provided in the resource section frequently have access to capital workshops or have contacts to refer you to. But here are a few things you should know before you go or decide to apply for funding:

- Ensure there is a true business need for it
- Have a solid/sound business plan prepared
- Ensure you know how much you need - some business owners make the mistake of not asking for enough
- Ensure you are pitch ready
- If you are a new business, ensure you have:
  - Good personal credit
  - Proof of your own assets and collateral
- If an existing business, ensure you have:
  - Good business credit
  - Good tax standing
  - Strong financials
  - The ability to repay
  - Proof of your own assets and collateral

If you need capital for your business either now or in the future,

1.  Do you have up to date business plans, financial statements, and growth strategies that show your financial strength and exactly what you need? If not, what do you need to do to prepare?

2.  What additional questions do you have about gaining access to capital?

**Protection**

There are a few different ways you need to think about being fully protected. As a business owner you need to ensure that:

- You and your family are protected
- Your staff is protected
- Your customers are protected
- Your intellectual property and ideas are protected

The three key people who can help you in the above scenarios are your:

- Insurance agent
- Financial planner
- Business attorney

Every company varies in terms of how it should protect itself based on its industry and sometimes even client requirements. For example, when it comes to business protection, medical doctors, truck drivers, and training consultants all have to carry completely different types and amounts of insurance. The key is that all three companies should be protected.

Are you fully covered in all areas of your life or business should something happen to you, a client or a staff member?

What do you need to do to ensure your confidence and security?

Be sure to check with your insurance agent, business attorney or financial planner annually to ensure that you are covered with the best protection.

# 9 UNDERSTANDING YOUR INDUSTRY

*"Sell the problem you solve not the product you sell." – Unknown*

Every industry has its pros and cons as it relates to business development. However, the industry overall might be impacted by current state laws, future trends, the economy, or other factors.
Yet the growth of your business will always be dependent on your understanding of:

1. The state of your industry
2. The state of your business

Understanding key industry and business functions will help you to speak your clients' language, ask relevant questions, participate fully in conversations, and truly act as a consultative partner.

Janice Bryant Howroyd is the founder and CEO of the Act-1 Group, the largest privately held woman-owned workforce solutions company, and the 1st African-American woman to own a billion-dollar company. You will often hear her tell her story of being born in the small town of Tarboro, NC and graduating from college with money pooled together by family and friends. Even though her start-up story includes launching with $1500, a fax machine, and humble beginnings, her billion-dollar story came from always following these ABC's of business.

1. **Ask** the right questions then listen
2. **Be** where you say you will be
3. **Circular** communication - In her company communication does not end with just hitting the send button of an email

Consistently following her ABC's of business has allowed her to not only understand her business and industry, but expand to 4 divisions in 19 countries.

Here's why it's important to know the state of your industry as well as the state of your business:

- An evolving industry with an antiquated business (model and products/services) = No Growth
- A stagnant industry whether your business is antiquated or a trendsetter = Little to no Growth
- An evolving industry with a competitive business model = Maximum Growth

**Key things to be aware of in your industry are:**
- Is it trending up, down or stabilizing?
- Is it saturated?
- Is it going to be impacted by external forces such as the economy? New laws? New technology?
- Do you have a competitive advantage to stand out from the crowd based on all of the above?

What is the current state of your industry?

What are the anticipated future trends?

How will your company meet those needs?

# 10 UNDERSTANDING YOUR TARGET MARKET

*"Most of your time should be spent learning about those who support you, not comparing yourself to your competition." - Melissa Nixon*

Understanding your target market such as their geography, age, education, hobbies, and buying patterns are critical to the growth and sustainability of your business. Knowing your target market helps to meet current needs as well as anticipate future needs with the creation of new products and services. In addition, investors, sponsors, and those you collaborate with will want to have confidence that you know how to get a return on their investment.

**Your Ideal Clients:**
Having a robust understanding of each of your client profiles helps you to know what they need, where to find them, and provide the right solutions for those needs. Most businesses have multiple ideal clients each with unique profiles based on their:

- Demographics
- Needs and pain points
- Goals

**Avatar Development:**
Let's take a look at your ideal client profiles by creating avatars, better known as buyer personas. Each buyer persona includes characteristics that map out your ideal customers story for you. Knowing your customers and target audience will:

1. Keep you focused
2. Help hone your messaging
3. Pinpoint specifically who you are marketing to and what their needs are

**Why have more than one avatar?**
Many businesses have more than avatar because they have more than one type of product or service for different customers. Each customer represents a story and a challenge that you have a solution for.

Look at an example avatar for a career consulting company and then complete your own for your company. The career consulting company is looking for ideal clients who need their services in times of displacement, job transition, or career advancement. Below you will see a description of what this type of client may look like. This helps the company know more about her so they know where and how to market to her.

## Avatar Example:

| Description: | Example: |
|---|---|
| Name: | Janice |
| Age: | 48 |
| Occupation: | HR Leader |
| Marital Status: | Married |
| # of Children: | 2 kids in college |
| Average Income: | 110K |
| Geography: | Georgia |
| Challenges: | Jane has excelled in her career and feels like she has reached a plateau. She feels like she is not walking in her purpose, is a little burned out in the corporate world, and seeking either a career change or exploring a business idea she has always had. She means well but always puts everyone else first instead of herself. |
| Hobbies/Pastimes: | She loves vacationing with her family, is heavily involved in her community, is an avid reader, and loves podcasts. |
| What they are looking for? Needs? | She is looking for inspiration, accountability, and direction on her next move. |
| What you offer? | Leadership and business coaching to guide her in the right direction. |

Now it's your turn? Describe two of your ideal clients below. Thinking through the persona of your ideal clients helps you with your marketing strategy, direction, and budget.

| Description: | Avatar #1: | Avatar #2: |
|---|---|---|
| Name: | | |
| Age: | | |
| Occupation: | | |
| Marital Status: | | |
| # of Children: | | |
| Income: | | |
| Geography: | | |
| Challenges: | | |
| Hobbies/ Pastimes: | | |
| What they are looking for? Needs? | | |
| What you offer? | | |

# 11 UNDERSTANDING YOUR PRODUCTS & SERVICES

*"So often people are working hard at the wrong thing. Working on the right thing is probably more important than working hard." – Caterina Fake, Co-founder, Flickr*

What you sell and how you sell it matters. Attracting clients is great when you have awesome marketing and messaging. However, retaining those clients only happens when you sell the right products and services that surpass the needs of your ideal clients.

The products and services you sell cannot be based upon:

- What *you* like, but should be based on what your customers need and like. Or what your friends and family think. However, what does customer research tell you?
- What others are doing - while knowing what your competitors are doing is great, your audience is *your* audience.
- What you've done in the past - your products or services should evolve with industry and economic trends as well as customer needs. When was the last time you introduced something new?

**List your top products and services below and share the results:**
Be sure to think about if what you are offering still works for your customers. When you think about the results, consider the following:

- How many people purchase it?
- How much time does it take to produce it compared to the value?
- How much does it cost you compared to the value?
- And lastly, if something needs to change, start thinking ahead about that change and when it needs to happen.

| Product/Service | Results: | What do you need to do differently? |
|---|---|---|
|  |  |  |
|  |  |  |
|  |  |  |

**Future Products & Services:**
What products or services do you need to launch within the next 6 - 12 months, if any?

| Product/Service | High Level Implementation Plan: |
|---|---|
|  |  |
|  |  |
|  |  |

Here is the one thing you will always see any successful business owner, brand, or influencer do when it comes to their products and services:

Get good at one thing first!

You see this most easily with influencer brands. Oprah, Jennifer Lopez, Beyoncé, and Ellen all become great at talk show hosting, singing, and comedy first. And then years after they built trusted and reliable brands, they expanded into to tv stations, clothing lines, food products, and home goods.

You will know it's time to shift and add to your product/service line when your customers' needs and wants change and when you've built trust with your audience.

# 12 UNDERSTANDING YOUR COMPETITION:

*"You are the difference maker in your industry. The moment you realize it will be the moment you will act like it." - Melissa Nixon*

In today's busy world, it is easy to be head down and focused on things that only pertain to your business. Most of the time we're barely making it through our long to do list before it's time to get up and do it all over again tomorrow. But one thing many business owners miss is understanding who their competition is at *all* times. It's something we only focus on during times of change such as when we are first starting our business, the economy is changing or the industry is changing.

You will often hear things like, "I am my own competition". Yes, you are. But you are also a smart CEO as well. To this day, retailers and restaurants still have secret shoppers, so why shouldn't you be aware of who others are and what they are doing in your industry? There's no need to be obsessed, but there should definitely be an awareness.

**What makes you stand out from the competition? Share your unique selling proposition:**
But here is where I want to stretch you, the keyword is *unique*? So, before you get started, think beyond typical things business owners

say like higher quality, faster service, etc. Every business promises those things. In addition to that, what makes your company, products, and services unique? Think about the following questions to help guide you.

Why do your clients choose you? Share what they have said, not what you think, such as feedback and testimonials.

What do you have or do that will make new clients choose you and existing clients stay?

Why should potential clients choose you instead of your competitors?

## List Your Top Competitors:

| Company Name | Location | Products/ Services | What is different about your company product or service? |
|---|---|---|---|
|  |  |  |  |
|  |  |  |  |
|  |  |  |  |
|  |  |  |  |

# 13 MARKETING

*"No one can buy what they don't know about."* -
*Melissa Nixon*

**M***arketing* is the story behind your brand and how you communicate with your potential and current customers. Without a solid marketing strategy, you work harder, not smarter. Referral based businesses are great, but new customers also exist outside of your referral network. Your marketing strategy should be noticeable and impactful throughout your entire client lifecycle. This approach not only allows you to attract the right clients but also retain and turn them into repeat clients.

You will hear terms like marketing, branding, advertising, and public relations. You will even hear the terms used interchangeably. However, marketing is always the overarching umbrella that consists of important activities such as branding, advertising, and PR.

Marketing is your way of *communicating* with your target audience throughout your client life cycle. There are many aspects of marketing, but here are four marketing elements your company should make plans to implement:

| Branding | The way you build and portray your company image to your audience |
|---|---|
| Social Media | How you communicate with your target audience through social networks |
| Advertising | How you promote or sell your products and services |
| Public Relations | How you build a relationship between your company and the public |

Each of the above elements is expected to work both independently and interdependently. All must work together to support the same marketing goal(s).

Your marketing strategy is critical because the more attracted potential customers are to your brand, the more you can build a relationship with them that leads to both conversion and retention.

In addition to having the marketing elements above, here are a few other marketing elements you should be sure to include in your marketing plans:

**Video Marketing**
Here's the honest truth. If your company is not doing some form of video marketing, you are behind the times. Video marketing is the #1-way companies are getting the word out about who they are, what they do, and what their client's experiences are. There are so many ways to use video these days from the quick use of your smartphone to social media live streaming that there is no excuse. At a minimum, your website should have a video that tells the story of your company and the value you provide.

Does your company currently use video marketing as a part of its marketing strategy?

To what extent does your company use video marketing in its marketing strategy? On a scale of 1 to 7, 1 = Not at all 7 = All the time

$$1 \quad 2 \quad 3 \quad 4 \quad 5 \quad 6 \quad 7$$

Video marketing can pay huge dividends such as an increase in brand awareness, relationship building, leads, and even new clients.

What's working about your current video marketing strategy?

What's not working?

What could you do differently?

Create a plan below to enhance your current video marketing strategy. Think about things such as where your target audience is located. As you create it, don't get overwhelmed. Remember you can take one video and syndicate it to the platforms that are appropriate for your audience.

### Video Marketing Plan:

| Platform: | Yes/No | How often? | What message will you share? |
|-----------|--------|------------|------------------------------|
| Website | | | |
| YouTube | | | |
| LinkedIn | | | |
| Facebook | | | |
| Instagram | | | |
| Other | | | |
| Other | | | |

## Company Website

You'd be surprised at the number of websites I see that are merely online business cards. A static site that only shares basic information such as your company names, products and services, and a way to contact you is an outdated way of doing business.

Your website should be an experience for your clients and potential clients. One that tells the story behind the company. Why? Because stories sell. Your site should also tell about your client experiences as well as provide a learning experience that includes things such as industry news and your content expertise.

Here are a few things to make sure you have a website that sells:

Our website...

- Has a video overview of our company
- Is constantly updated with new content
- Has updated client testimonials
- Has a way for our customers to opt into our email lists

How satisfied are you with your current website on a scale of 1 to 7, 1 being very dissatisfied and 7 being very satisfied?

1   2   3   4   5   6   7

What would you like to see done differently? List below.

How would those changes help with your client experience and client conversion?

Describe your plan below to create a more sales oriented and customer-oriented site. Share things like your estimated deadline to complete. How much it will cost? How long it will take? Who will do it and when?

## Email Marketing & Automation

You'd also be surprised at the number of companies that do not have an email list or if they do, they do not communicate regularly with their email list.

A potential and current clients email address = REVENUE!

Here are a few things you should think about when it comes to your email marketing campaign:

- New and creative list-building strategies
- Your average email open rate - Industry standards state that a 30% open rate is great
- Savvy email subject titles to cause your list to hit the open button
- The type of content you include
- The frequency of communication
- Ensuring there is a balance between sharing value-added content and asking for sales
- Your funnel and follow-up strategy

How effective is your email marketing strategy? On a scale of 1 to 7, 1 being not effective and 7 being very effective.

1    2    3    4    5    6    7

What enhancements can you implement into your email marketing? List below.

How would these changes help with your overall marketing strategy, client experience, and client conversion?

Describe your plan below to create a more effective email marketing strategy. Share things like your estimated deadline to complete. How much it will cost? How long will it take? Who will do it and when?

**All marketing is not good marketing**

Social media is a catalyst for an increase in business success for entrepreneurs in recent years by providing ease of access to ideal clients. However, consumers can also share their thoughts about your business to the world, good or bad, with the click of a button. For major industries such as retailers, airlines, and hotels they have entire teams online every day ready to respond to customer complaints, manage the brand's reputation, and accommodate them as best as they can. Can't get through to a 1-800 number? No worries, just send a tweet for a quick response. Didn't like your hotel stay, don't worry, just hop on TripAdvisor to be acknowledged and heard.

But how should you handle it if and when it happens to your small business? The great thing about small businesses is that they are small and you can quickly react to customer complaints or negative press.

**Here are a few tips to help with handling customer complaints or negative publicity:**

- Operate with integrity - do and deliver what you say you would in the timeframe you said you would with the quality you said you would. It's hard for people to say anything negative when you have delivered on your brand promise.
- Operate within your capacity - growth is what we all want but it's when demand exceeds our capacity that we begin to fail on what we promised our customers.
- Be sure to regularly check social media and email accounts. Nothing makes a situation worse than having an ignored problem.
- If possible, contact the customer directly via phone or email to resolve the issue 1:1
- It can be easy to be defensive to protect your brand but the #1 thing you can immediately do is listen and understand the customer's point of view (whether they are right or wrong).
- Continuously share great brand stories such as testimonials, acts of service, etc. so if there ever is negative publicity or customer complaints, you will have already established a strong brand reputation and trust.
- Always offer to accommodate customers for any inconvenience. Ask not just what they want, but what would make the situation right for them.
- In cases of national media attention or viral news, immediately consult a PR expert/company.

Here is a personal story of a great example of how a company handled a bad situation. One year, I planned a big milestone birthday party. It was on a lake, an all-white theme, catered with my favorite foods, with 40 of my closest friends and family. The only problem was that the caterer was a no show. No record of our order, no one on the way to feed 40 hungry guests who were at the lake house hungry and ready to have a great time. Talk about a disaster! Thankfully we saved the day with last minute restaurant orders. But the caterer did all of the above steps and went above and beyond to rectify the situation after the party. From emails, phone calls, personally delivering a reimbursement check to my door, to compensating me with a comparable catering experience for a future date, they did everything they could to course correct the mistake.

# 14 BUSINESS & PERSONAL BRANDING

*"In order to be irreplaceable, one must always be different." - Coco Chanel*

Your brand is more than your logo or even your company colors. It is inclusive of any and everything your target audience experiences whenever they interact with your company. It is an ongoing relationship you have with your potential and current customers. Every time you consistently show up in the marketplace further strengthens your relationship with your customers. It says this is a brand I can *trust*. Here are 8 branding elements to assess your market presence, adapted from brandanew.co.

| Element: | 8 Branding Elements and What They Mean |
|---|---|
| Brand Identity | These are easily identifiable factors such as a company name, logo, etc. What visuals come to mind when you think of Apple, Nike, or even McDonalds? |
| Brand Image | This is the image and expected experience that comes to mind when your target audience thinks about you. What image comes to mind when you |

| | |
|---|---|
| | think of Nordstrom? Or Tiffany & Co.? |
| Brand Positioning | Your brand position refers to what segment of the market you will focus on in your company. When you think of fast food - Chick-Fil-a, McDonald's, and Chipotle all have different market segments, positions, and even price points. |
| Brand Personality | Your company's brand personality is no different than our personalities. Funny, serious, light-hearted, playful, straight to the point...you name it. Your company's brand personality comes across in everything that is communicated with your audience such as the look, feel, and messaging. |
| Brand Experience | This is the entire experience your audience has with your brand from the time they hear about it. What do they see? What do they hear through your messaging? How are they treated? What does the packaging look like? How fast is service? |
| Brand Differentiation | What makes you different and stand out? Think about Chick-Fil-a customer service. Many consumers have never had a bad experience with the brand. |
| Brand Communication | What's your message? Is it clear who you are, what you sell, and what you stand for? |
| Brand Extension | Once your brand is well established you can introduce extensions to your brand. Celebrities become known for the craft of singing, acting or dancing, then they introduce new brand extensions of perfume, clothing and home decor. |

Each element is important to your brand strength. However, people's first interaction with your company is either going to be what others are saying about your brand or your brand image. It is the element that causes them to judge all other components about your business such as customer service, product/service quality, and more. It is also a key decision point as to whether customers, supporters or future partners want to start a relationship with you or not. I will never forget driving down a major interstate when I saw an 18-wheeler and underneath the company name and logo the truck said, *"A Native-American Woman Owned Business."* Talk about impressive. I was so impressed that I emailed the company owner. That is what great branding does, starts relationships with those who are supposed to be in your network. After researching her company, a little more, I have also shared her brand story and business with others. All from a 60-second citing of one of her trucks on the interstate. What does your brand image prompt others to do for you?

**Your Brand Strength**
Based on those elements how strong is your brand and what can you do to enhance it?

| Element: | Brand Strength: |
|---|---|
| Brand Identity | |
| Brand Image | |
| Brand Positioning | |
| Brand Personality | |
| Brand Experience | |
| Brand Differentiation | |
| Brand Communication | |
| Brand Extension | |

*"Your smile is your business, your personality is your business card, how you leave others feeling after an experience with you becomes your trademark!" -*
*Unknown*

## Personal Branding

As the CEO of your company, the first thing you have to remember about branding is that *you are the brand.*

When people meet you, they meet the brand. It doesn't matter how great your website is, how great your team is, or what results you have achieved in the past. All that matters is *you* in that moment.

**In the few moments of interacting with others, people notice:**
- Your Appearance (Hair, apparel, cleanliness)
- Your Attitude (Confidence and disposition)
- Your Actions (What you say and what you do)

**What they experience with you determines:**
- Whether there will be a purchase
- Whether there will be a next meeting or a follow-up phone call or email
- Whether they will refer you or pass along your name
- Whether they think you are qualified

**When you think of your personal brand, what works well?**

What would you like to change?

Based on those changes, what will you do next and when?

*"Personal Branding is a LEADERSHIP Requirement,*
*not a self-promotion campaign." – Forbes*

# 15 SALES & REVENUE

*"If your dreams don't scare you, then they're too small" - Richard Branson*

There are plenty of sales funnel models. Most of them might have anywhere from three to eight steps. But because every business model is different in how they execute their sales funnels, we'll stick to the basics of generating leads, converting leads to customers and client retention.

## Generating Leads

Where do most of your leads come from? Fyi, referral-based businesses are great, however, every company should have a lead generation process that generates organic leads.

| Lead Source<br>i.e. website | Percentage<br>i.e. 40% |
|---|---|
|  |  |
|  |  |

|  |  |
| --- | --- |
|  |  |

**Based on your responses:**
What's working well that you need to do more of?

What's not working that you should stop?

What's missing that you need to add?

**Converting Leads to Clients**
Leads are great because leads indicate a strong source of potential revenue. Keyword *potential*. Now it's a matter of how you turn these leads into clients. Here are a few key factors that need to be aligned in order to make that happen:

- Clarity about who are you and what you can do for them
- The right product or service to solve the potential client's needs
- The right price
- The right time
- The right quality
- Relationship and trust
- Making the ask - not all clients know what they need until they are told and extended an offer

What percentage of your leads do you typically convert to clients?

How long is your sales cycle from lead generation to client conversion?

How does this compare to your industry average?

Is there anything you can start or stop to shorten the sales cycle?

When you think about your current clients, why did they choose you?

For those deals that you did not convert, what do you think prevented them from moving forward?

## Client Retention

Client retention is dependent upon several factors as well:

- **Loyalty** - Loyal clients will not be easily swayed by other competitors even if they are more cost efficient, have a bigger brand, etc. People prefer relationships.
- **Relationship** - Your client experience should not just be focused on excellent delivery of your product or service, but also your great relationship.
- **Value -** Clients will only stay if they feel like there is a good exchange of value, quality, and experience for their investment.
- **Awareness -** Clients only know what you tell and show them. But often times your company provides much more than they are aware of, however, it is your job to create that level of awareness and meet their needs.

The biggest mistake most of us make is staying too focused on the first two parts of the sales funnel process, lead generation, and conversion. As a result, the development of a robust client experience is neglected.

Does your company have a client experience process or map that you or someone on your team follows?

Here are some questions and tips to help you build your own client experience map if not:

What happens once a person or company becomes a lead? List all the steps below.

What happens once a person or company becomes a client? List all the steps below.

Listed below are some examples of great relationship building touchpoints that could lead to client retention, contract renewal or returning customers:

- Over delivery
- Client anniversary with your company
- Thinking of you cards or gifts
    - Client's business anniversary
    - Birthday
    - Business or personal achievement
    - Holiday cards
- Business development
    - Send news articles on industry trends or something you are working on
    - Touch base meetings to understand their biggest challenge (great for service-based industries such as consultants)

There are plenty of company's whom you have purchased a product or service from and never heard from them again. Your goal is to *never* be that company. Treat your potential clients in such a way that they look forward to hearing from you and always have a reason to come back.

# 16 PRICING

*"Nobody talks about entrepreneurship as a survival, but that's exactly what it is and what nurtures creative thinking. Running that first shop taught me business is not financial science; it's about trading: buying and selling." - Anita Roddick, Founder of The Body Shop*

Sales, pricing and profitability require an intentional strategy and business model. Successful businesses pick a position in the marketplace and follow the rules within their pricing strategy no matter what happens in the market such as an economic downturn or an economic surplus. For example, have you ever heard of a sale at Tiffany & Co? No.

There are a number of pricing strategies that brands employ, here are just a few adapted from quickbooks.intuit.com:

- Core Values - No matter the economy, Chick-fil-a is always closed on Sundays
- Discount Pricing - For years Wal-Mart has had a marketing campaign for "falling prices"
- Premium Pricing - Tiffany's will always be premium priced, their trademarked baby blue bag is not available for sale unless you make a purchase

- Value Pricing - Sign up today and get "x" amount of dollars, products or services in bonuses
- Bulk Pricing - Sometimes you need all eight jumbo kinds of Ketchups from Sam's Club or BJs
- Competitive Pricing - We accept competitor coupons. Your customers know you will always be within a reasonable range of the next competitor

The key to a successful pricing strategy is knowing *your* customers and consistency. In the beginning, you may test certain marketing strategies, but over time consistency is what builds trust with your customers.

**Determine your pricing strategy**
This is the easier of the two questions because honestly there is no right answer. Here are a few things to consider when creating your pricing strategy:

- Your target markets.
- The quality and value of your product or service.
- What your industry, target market and the economy can withstand?
- What are you and/or your company's core values?
- What type of clients do you want to attract?
- How much profit margin do you desire to have?

**When to change your pricing strategy?**
This will be determined by the type of change you desire to make and the purpose for that change. For example, it will be a hard sell to go from a discount brand to a premium-priced brand. These are two very different audiences. But when you do decide to change or pivot here are some things to consider:

- Offer a tier pricing approach by introducing new products or services. However, this will only be effective if the new prices are closely aligned with your current price point.
- Launch new products or services possibly under a different brand name. For example, a Nissan Sentra and Infinity are both made by Nissan. This will be needed if you want to

introduce a pricing strategy that is opposite to what your customers are used to.

**Price Strategy Implementation:**
What is your current pricing strategy?

How did you determine your current price strategy?

How is your current price strategy working for your company?

In the next 12 - 24 months, will your price strategy stay the same or change? If so, how?

# 17 PROFITABILITY

*"People say that money is not the key to happiness,
but I always figured if you have enough money you
can have a key made." - Joan Rivers*

Your sales funnel and pricing processes are great lead indicators for setting goals and determining how much revenue you want to make. Now, the question is how much do you want to keep?

What do you need to do to be more profitable and keep more of the revenue you are making in the business? There are several things to consider. Is it a...

- Quantity issue? If you converted more leads and retained more clients in your sales funnel would your profits increase?
- Expense issue? Some companies increase their profits simply by analyzing and reducing their expenses. This can be easy decisions such as cutting back on the cost of supplies to much harder ones like looking at headcount.
- Product or service issue? Are there new products or services you could be offering to your clients?
- Price issue? Companies have been willing to lose a portion of their customers by increasing their prices. In return, they doubled their sales as result and increased their bottom line.

- Brand issue? Brand perception is everything especially today with so much opportunity at your client's fingertips to share about their experiences.
- Finance issue? Sometimes things such as the wrong type of company set up or tax designation can impact your profitability as well.

When you think about what can increase your profits, what are the top two or three things you and your team could do differently?

1. _____
   _____
   _____

2. _____
   _____
   _____

3. _____
   _____
   _____

# 18 UNDERSTANDING YOUR FINANCIALS

*"Do what you have to until you can do what you
want to." - Oprah Winfrey*

Remember when I asked who's on your team? Well, that team should always include a CPA, bookkeeper, and a financial planner. These roles are especially critical for business owners in making decisions that will make your business even more successful and marketable.

Understanding your financials is essential in order for you to understand your business story as well as to:

- Understand your cash flow
- Understand your capacity for growth
- Make strategic business decisions
- Gain access to capital
- Be a strong contender for a joint venture partnership
- Share your financial strength and future with potential investors
- Selling your company

Many business owners long for contracts, partnerships, and opportunities with major brands. They can only imagine the day when they can get their products in stores such as Wal-Mart or endorsed by Oprah for the "Oprah Effect." Everything in life changes once this happens right? Possibly. Or it could be so short-lived because you were not prepared financially or operationally for the influx of sales or success. Many small business owners are often disappointed by being told no from the major conglomerate's multiple times. But rightfully so because they would much rather protect both you and them.

But one of the things major brands can do before giving you a contract is give you a chance. This can come in the form of helping to create awareness for your product or service, developing you and/or your team, or even giving you access to others you may need to know in their network. This is what happened to Tracy, owner of one of the most delicious pound cake companies in the Southeast. A C-suites executive from a major bank tasted her product at an event and loved it. Her response was not, let me introduce you to the right people to get you a loan. But instead, she created access and allowed her to provide the dessert for an upcoming meeting that included a number of executives from other major companies. One of those companies was Walmart who also loved her product. Their response to her product was amazing. Again, not a scenario where they immediately said let's put your product in our stores but instead, "Let's take a look at your business." Both scenarios provided her great access and opportunity versus setting her up for failure.

Even with a great product, they still needed to assess her financial strength and viability, even if her product was only going to be tested in a few stores. She needed to know:

- How much supplies she would need?
- How much demand could she realistically keep up with?
- Will she be able to deliver in a timely fashion?
- Does she have the physical space to handle the increased orders?
- Can her business withstand the profit margin she will ultimately make?
- Can her business model withstand the payment terms?
- Does the deal allow enough profit margin?

I always ask new and existing businesses, "If an investor or major brand approached you today, would you be ready?" While numbers may not be fun to some, they are the precursor to your next level of success.

There are plenty of financial statements and ratios which can be overwhelming. But have a conversation with your CPA to review the following statements. This will help you to understand your financial position and future better than anything else.

- Income statement
- Balance sheet
- Statement of cash flows
- Statement of retained earnings

Combined, these statements paint a clear picture of: 1) the story of your business and 2) the health of your business. But here are a few mistakes some business owners make when it relates to their financials:

- Not taking the time to learn
- Trusting others to figure it out for them
- Not reviewing them on a regular basis

On a scale of 1 to 7, how confident are you in understanding the financial health of your company? 1 = not confident at all; 7 = very confident

1    2    3    4    6    7

What areas of your company's financial health do you need to understand more of?

Who can you leverage as a resource to help?

# 19 BUSINESS DEVELOPMENT & FORECASTING

*"Courage is a repetitive action."- Melissa Nixon*

Business Development is the *heartbeat* of your business! Many business owners are known for working *in* their business versus *on* their business. On any given day there are a myriad of administrative and marketing activities to do. However, unless what you are working on is an *"income-producing or growth"* activity revolving around the prospecting, follow-up of a sale, or growth of your business, it's not business development.

### Examples of what business development is and is not:

| Business Development is... | Business Development is not... |
|---|---|
| Gaining leads at networking events | Working on your website or doing actual client work *(unless it will create more leads/sales)* |
| Following-up with a hot prospect via phone or email | Working on your social media *(unless it will create more leads/sales)* |
| Taking a prospective client to lunch or coffee | Researching on the internet |
| Hosting/participating in | Working on your business finances |

| events where prospects learn more about your services | |
| --- | --- |
| Strategy planning sessions | A host of busy conference calls/meetings |

**Top 10 Business Development Mistakes:**
1. Being too passive
2. Not asking for the sale
3. Waiting for others to suggest a sale or suggest to work with you
4. Being priced too low
5. Emailing vs picking up the phone
6. Not telling people what they need
7. Not consistently including a CTA "call to action" in everything you do
8. Not knowing your numbers
9. Not knowing your capacity to take on new business
10. *NOT FOLLOWING UP!*

**Biz Development Tip:** Small business owners are often the CEO, "Chief of Everything". Creating a weekly process to set aside time to do each of your activities is a sure way to win.

What do you need to do less of to focus more on income-producing activities?

What do you need to do more of to focus on incoming-producing activities?

**What bold steps can you take to grow your revenue in the next:**
24 hours?

7 days?

30 days?

Forecasting is the process that allows you to see into the future of your business to make the best strategic decisions.

Business forecast involves two primary methods:

- Qualitative
- Quantitative

This process always helps to answer your questions of curiosity such as, "Will a particular target market buy more or less of a certain product that I sell?" The answer to that question should be based more on research than your best-educated guess. It should be based either on qualitative market research or on your actual numbers. Your results will never be 100% accurate because the future isn't here yet, but they can definitely act as a guide in your decision-making process of the following:

- How much product to buy?
- What changes do I need to make to:
    o Our offerings
    o Our brand
    o Our expenses
- How much space is needed?
- How much staff do I need?

You should be able to make strategic business decisions based on what you anticipate the following financial results to be:

- Expenses
- Revenue

**Why forecasting is beneficial for your business?**
- Your business model, goals and plans may change, but your business plan and forecast are your roadmaps for success
- Every business should have a forecasted budget based on past history and future expectations
- No business should be caught off guard financially if they develop the discipline and practice of looking ahead
- Business owners who budget and forecast have more time to be strategic versus putting out fires

**When you look ahead to the next 12 - 24 months what are some anticipated changes you can see in the following?**

Revenue:

Expenses:

Product/Service Offerings:

Industry:

# 20 JOINT VENTURES & COLLABORATIONS

*"If you are offered a seat on a rocket ship, you don't ask what seat? You just get on." - Sheryl Sandberg*

Sometimes the easiest way to be a star is to shine with other people. It's not something many business owners and solopreneurs want to hear; but in many cases, it's true. We are better together. This is especially the case if you have a focus for targeting larger corporations or want to make a bigger impact in general.

One of my favorite hair care lines is Carol's Daughter, a minority-owned company, started by Lisa Price in New York City. I can remember years ago visiting her flagship store on our NYC things to do list. I was even more excited when her products became available in Macy's and eventually Target. Not only because of the accessibility of Carol's Daughter products but because of Lisa's success in growing her business. But that type of success and growth is not easily achieved or maintained. I can imagine her having a vision for what's next but not sure how to get there. Every major leap of growth requires more capital, more assets, and more resources than it took to reach the last level. As popular as the brand was, competitors increased, sales declined, and the company eventually filed for bankruptcy. It's at those moments business owners have to ask themselves is this about holding on to the brand that I built or preserving the legacy of the brand? Lisa could have stayed self-focused and said it is more important for Carol's Daughter to remain a minority-owned company. Or she could decide to preserve the brand by becoming a member of the retail conglomerate, L'Oréal, which she did. That decision not only preserved the brand but it expanded it to now over 30K retail stores across the country.

> *Coming together is a beginning. Keeping together is progress. Working together is success." -Henry Ford*

Have you experienced a joint venture or even considered it? Why or why not?

## Purpose of Joint Ventures & Collaborations:
1. Increase in Visibility
2. Increase in Revenue
3. Increase in Profit
4. Increase in Thought Partnership (Strategy & Direction)
5. Increase in Support

## Ideal Scenarios for JVs & Collaboration:
- Corporate Contracts
- Government Contracts
- Brand Expansion
- Company Growth

Joint ventures and collaborations may sound like a great idea, but with who? Trust has to be the number one factor or it will not work. Here are 7 traits of an ideal partner.

Someone who...

- Works as hard as you do
- Shares the same vision
- Compliments your skillset

- Is dependable
- Treats customers, programs, products, etc. like their own
- Feels like an addition to the team, not a burden
- Creates clarity, not confusion

In what areas of your business could you use additional support such as a joint venture or collaboration?

What are a few next steps toward creating that partnership? Who are some potential partners that come to mind or you could ask for a referral?

*"None of us is as smart as all of us." - Ken Blanchard*

# 21 LAUNCHING A NEW PRODUCT OR SERVICE

*"I'm not afraid of failure; I'm afraid of regret" -*
*Melissa Nixon*

Launching a new product, service or even a business is a big deal that warrants a lot of attention. Beyoncé is the only person who has the ability to secretly drop albums in a wildly successful way. You, on the other hand, should shout your news from the mountain tops! But the mistake most people make is taking on the mentality to make major moves in silence. That is also the quickest way to let the product or service silently die.

I remember when we launched our consulting firm, a marketing expert told me, "You have to take people on the journey with you" during our launch process. It was the best marketing advice I received to date. Your customers and followers want to be a part of the process. They are excited to grow with you. In addition, taking them on the journey allows them to further build a trustworthy relationship with you and the new product or service.

In instances when you cannot reveal too much information because it's still in development, there are still ways to market indirectly. Here are few ways to help you tell the story, create anticipation and turn your followers into buyers:

- Share teaser emails, social media posts, videos, etc. letting your followers know that something is coming or stay tuned

for me
- Do a countdown to the big reveal
- Engage your audience in the process. Poll them to let them help you choose things like logos, colors, fonts, book covers, etc. I remember we did a book cover contest for my first book. Guess what? The cover I liked was different than the cover that won the majority vote
- Depending on what it is, you can do things like creating a virtual launch team to help spread the word
- If you choose to use a launch team, you can have people play specific roles. For example, colleagues that have large email lists could share their lists. Followers that are great with video could be an ambassador to do a video for you
- You can also consider hosting an in-person or virtual launch party

Each of these are ideas that enable your followers and clients to feel a part of the process and creates even greater advocates. You will get much further traction with being consistent in the things above than silently creating a big reveal to the market...unless you are Beyoncé of course.

Each new product or service you offer should have a launch/plan strategy that includes the following:

- A calendar noting your pre, during, and post-launch activities
- Email Sequence - start thinking about compelling copy
- Social Media Plan - don't forget video is IN
- Launch/Ambassador team, optional. You will have to think through what's in it for them and what additional you can give them of value if you choose this option

How long should your launch process be? It depends on several factors such as the product, price point, industry, economy, target audience and more. In my industry, a conference can take up to a year to plan, market, and execute compared to 60 – 90 days for other products and services. You will have to determine how long it will take to build brand awareness and then convert that awareness to buying customers.

Do you have a new product or service launching soon? Start drafting out your launch plans/ideas in the white space below.

# Notes & Reflections

# For Her Leadership

Melissa J. Nixon

# 22 PROFESSIONAL & PERSONAL DEVELOPMENT

*"Change is inevitable. Growth is optional."*
*- John Maxwell*

Again, the biggest mistake business owners make is working *in* their business and not *on* their business...better yet, even on themselves. The best assessment you can do for your business is to ask:

## "How am I growing?"

What are you doing to take care of yourself both personally and professionally? The key areas every business owner should have both a pulse check on and a plan for growth/improvement are professional development, health, spiritual, emotional and family.

For astrophysicist, Dr. Jedidah Isler, Founder of the non-profit STEM en Route to Change (SeRCH) Foundation, Inc, her personal and professional development comes in a number of ways. Even with a demanding academic career and running SeRCH which is dedicated to using STEM as a pathway for social justice, she still finds time to make growth and development a priority. One of her favorite pastimes is reading in which she challenges herself to see how many books she can read in a year. When is the last time you read 30 books in 12 months?

On a scale of 1- 7, rate how you are doing when it comes to

intentional growth and development in each of the following areas. 1 = Not intentional at All 7 = Very Intentional

| | | | | | | | |
|---|---|---|---|---|---|---|---|
| Professional Development | 1 | 2 | 3 | 4 | 5 | 6 | 7 |
| Health | 1 | 2 | 3 | 4 | 5 | 6 | 7 |
| Spiritual | 1 | 2 | 3 | 4 | 5 | 6 | 7 |
| Emotional | 1 | 2 | 3 | 4 | 5 | 6 | 7 |
| Family | 1 | 2 | 3 | 4 | 5 | 6 | 7 |

Another common mistake is trying to create total life and business transformation simultaneously. If you have not been to a professional development conference in 10 years, it's hard to commit to doing something monthly, right? But what you can do is plan and say, this is what I can commit to for the following quarter or year.

Let's get intentional and create a plan of growth for you. For each area, write down one or two things you can do differently to begin to change this area of your life and business.

### Plan of Growth:

| Area of Development | Plan of Growth |
|---|---|
| Professional Development | i.e. What conferences will you attend? What associations will you become affiliated with? |
| Health | |
| Spiritual | |
| Emotional | |
| Family | |
| Other | |
| Other | |

Based on that list what are the top two or three things you commit to doing in the next 30 days?

Balance has been overrated and hard to achieve simply because it's hard to be all things to all people. it is difficult because it is hard to give yourself permission to be 100% present to the thing or person that needs you the most in that moment. This also means that something or someone else may have to wait for your full undivided attention in moments when you need to take care of yourself.

It is not about creating balance but managing your priorities and eliminating excuses:

- For you not to be in your best health, find the time.
- For your family to feel like they are on the back burner because you are always working, find the time.
- For you not to grow or be a top expert in your industry because you don't have time to attend conferences, etc., find the time.
- For you not to be at your best spiritually or emotionally because you don't have time to go to church, meditate, or therapy when needed, find the time.

# 23 BECOMING A THOUGHT LEADER IN YOUR INDUSTRY

*"Thought leadership is the boldness to say what needs to be said, not what everyone else is saying. And then teach others more about it."- Melissa Nixon*

Are you a thought leader in your industry? Someone who is seen as an authority figure, an expert or influencer? One way to make your business stand out in your industry and set yourself apart from competitors is to become a thought leader. The person who is leading the way, sharing valuable content and teaching others not only best practices but also future trends. Becoming a thought leader means you come out from behind the scenes of your company into the public eye where you can teach others what you know. It is a great way to not only build your personal brand but create awareness around your business brand.

Even if you answered "no" to being a thought leader at this juncture, but you want to be, it can be done. In today's online environment the world really is your oyster. But where do you start and how do you continue to grow your visibility? You can do this by,

- Sharing value-added content via your company website
- Speaking at industry conferences
- Speaking for professional associations - both regional and national

- Writing for industry and professional association magazines
- Publishing your writing on sites such as LinkedIn, Medium and the Huffington Post
- Being a guest contributor for major blogs and publications
- Doing interviews on reputable podcasts and other online shows
- TV and news appearances
- Write a book(s)

Becoming a thought leader doesn't just happen; it takes work on your part. It will require that you are:

- Willing to teach others
- Willing to share different or cutting edge thought philosophies
- Being visible
- Being consistent
- Using your voice
- Pushing the envelope
- A mentor

It also takes systems. Gaining visibility and credibility is great, but it can also be time wasted if your company is not ready for the influx of followers, inquiries, and sales. Things to consider once you start becoming a thought leader in your industry:

- How will people be able to get in contact with you when they read your article or see you on TV?
- What is the social media experience new followers will have when they start following you?
- What is the website experience potential new clients will have when they visit your site?
- Are you prepared with the products and services they are looking for?

Let's get visible! As a thought leader, what is it that you want to be known for?

Share your overarching message below:

Share 3 key points that support your message:

List the best places you can share your message and expertise

| Media Outlet Type: | Name(s): |
|---|---|
| Social Media | |
| Conferences | |
| Associations | |
| Publications | |
| Podcasts | |
| TV | |
| Radio | |
| Blogs | |

Honestly, it's hard to be all places at one time. Whether or not you are just getting started or looking to expand your influence, having a strategy is key.

**Share below the top three places you would like to share your message over the next 6 months:**

Whether or not you desire to be a thought leader in your industry, you definitely should be visible and using your voice. Truthfully, it's not an option. Why? Because you can't be the best-kept secret in your industry.

## Speaking

One of the best ways to become and be seen as a thought-leader is through speaking. For years, speaking has been left to motivational speakers who do amazing keynotes. While they are still around, many conferences and associations are looking for industry experts just like yourself to take the stage. So, if you have ever had a desire to speak, now is the time.

Whether this is your 1st or 50th talk, here are a few ways to prepare, to create an engaging experience.

What is your compelling message? What do you desire to share with the audience?

Share 3 topics/titles you could share at an upcoming conference or workshop?

1.

2.

3.

For each topic, what would be the 3 key takeaways for your audience?

| Title: | Key Takeaways: |
|---|---|
| | 1.<br><br>2.<br><br>3. |
| | 1.<br><br>2.<br><br>3. |
| | 1.<br><br>2.<br><br>3. |

Each key takeaway should have a compelling story. Every point should have a story and every story should have a point. What stories can you incorporate to engage the audience?

| Title: | Engaging Stories |
|---|---|
| | 1.<br><br>2.<br><br>3. |
| | 1.<br><br>2.<br><br>3. |

| | 1. |
|---|---|
| | 2. |
| | 3. |

Describe how you want your audience to feel at the end of your talk? i.e. inspired, informed, challenged, etc.

Speaking more not only begins to elevate you as a thought leader, but it is also a form of marketing. Here a few key things to remember...

- Before each talk, always think about what you want your desired outcome to be. Are you looking for leads? Clients? Partnerships? Visibility?
- Ensure you have the right systems and processes in place based on what you want your desired outcome to be. If you want leads or clients, how will you get them? What is your follow-up process?
- Seed your talk with client experiences. I've been in sessions where talking about client experiences has been overkill. But there is a way to do it subtly without sounding like a sleazy salesman.

# 24 COMPANY CULTURE

*"A leader is one who knows the way, shows the way, goes the way." - John Maxwell*

Another area many business owners often overlook is their company culture. Whether you are a solopreneur or have a staff of 100+, your company culture will be a critical factor to both the talent and customers you attract and retain.

Your company has a culture that was either developed intentionally or systematically over time.

It's created by:

- Your brand image and personality
- Your company core values
- Your company's mission and vision
- How you treat your potential and existing customers
- How you treat your staff
- Your best practices (or not)

Everything you do in business creates your culture. The best companies do not just let their culture organically evolve; it is intentionally created. This happens by analyzing:

- Systems and processes
- Training & Development
- Leadership Behavior

Here are a few questions to help you intentionally set your company's culture:

How would you describe your current company culture?

What do you want others to say about your company culture?

What do you and your team need to start, stop or improve in order to make that happen?

# 25 TEAM DEVELOPMENT

*"Leadership is not being in charge. Leadership is about taking care of those in your charge."*
*- Simon Sinek*

Earlier in the playbook we talked about who's on your team. In order to develop a powerhouse high-performing team, they must be developed. That should not just be the goal of Ashley Lamothe, but every business owner. Ashley started her career with Chick-fil-A at the age of 15 and became the youngest women to become an owner of a Chick-fil-A franchise at the age of 26.

As she transitioned to franchise owner she said her passion was to help her team grow. "I want to help them get to where they want to go, whether it's a career with Chick-fil-A, or studying law or medicine, or anything. I want to help them make that next step, just like so many have done for me."

There is no better outlook on people development than this. It is also the right perspective compared to the following when:

The CFO asks the CEO, "What happens if we invest in our people and then they leave us?"

The CEO asks the CFO, "What happens if we don't and they stay?"

This can be a sensitive matter and should be approached thoughtfully. However, there are many resources to help navigate your team's development from free online help to seeking help from an executive coach.

Here are some things to think about before you make development decisions:

What are my company's biggest needs right now?

How soon do you need that skill set?

Is it something that someone existing on the team can learn? Or is it something you need to hire internally (externally) for (full-time, part-time or 1099) or outsource?

If internal, who? If external, when will you do it?

How much is in your budget for internal staff development?

What are the best development opportunities to develop that skill set? List below based on your development budget.

| | |
|---|---|
| Free | (Articles, YouTube, Tutorials) |
| Low Costs | (Books, workbooks, book clubs) |
| Mid Costs | (Conferences and workshops) |
| Premium | (High-end coaching, certification, retreats) |

# 26 WHAT SUCCESSFUL CEOS DO

*"The road to **success** and the road to failure are almost exactly the same." - Colin R. Davis*

If you are using this resource guide as a tool, then I'm sure somewhere along your journey you have read an article or two on the top 5 things successful CEOs do in magazines such as Forbes, Entrepreneur and INC. Each article is an interview of highly successful CEOs and business owners on the repetitive attitude, behaviors, and traits that have gotten them to where they are.

To be honest, there are a lot of behaviors, attitudes, and traits that can make a person successful, not just a top 5 or a top 10. It simply comes down to what positive habits and rituals YOU create and follow for yourself as CEO...relentlessly! Your strategy will be the only one that works for you and your business.

What current habits or practices do you follow that has contributed to your current success level?

Here is a list of a few habits and rituals successful CEOs do...

- Early bedtime
- Early wake-up time
- Morning routine
- Daily exercise
- Healthy eating

- Reflection/Quiet Time
- Saying No
- Setting Goals
- Reviewing the next day, the night before
- Prayer or Meditation
- Serving others
- Limited email/screen time
- Vacation
- Values that are non-negotiable

What habits and rituals would you like to add to your current routine?

What is getting in your way from starting or continuing them? What do you need to do differently?

# 27 MINDSET AND MENTAL HEALTH

*"Vulnerability is the birthplace of innovation, creativity and change." - Brene Brown*

The #1 thing that can keep a business owner from achieving the business of their dreams, is that business owner's own stinking thinking! It's not the people, resources, financial, systems or even visibility. Self-assured leaders know how to do two things...fail forward or pivot to course correct. But operating in self-sabotaging behaviors is not their mode of operation.

Operating a business with a negative mindset does two things:

1. Allows whatever to happen in their life or business to become a self-fulfilling prophecy
2. Provides rationale for the reason the self-fulling prophecy happened. It can become a never-ending cycle that leaves your business stagnant with minimal growth if you're not careful.

Imagine if your day was continually filled with thoughts like this:

- No one knows about us because I'm not good at marketing and can't afford to hire a marketing team

- People only do business with those they know, like and trust and no one really knows about us
- We can't win that contract because we are not big enough yet

So, what is getting in your way? What are the thoughts you tell yourself or think about yourself and your business that are not true? List them below...all of them...even the ones you have never told anyone before.

Can I ask you a question? Where did these thoughts come from? If we know the things we are saying to ourselves and others about us are not true, why are you saying it? Thinking it? Or most importantly believing it? Share below. For each thought, try to think back and share when you started thinking it and why?

The most successful CEOs are confident, secure, and self-assured. But they have only gotten there after dealing with years of failure, rejection, and risk taking. Even when they are not, they have developed the right skill sets and resiliency to know how to reframe, refocus, and move on. They learned over time that mistakes happen and failure is a part of business; both making them stronger as people and leaders.

This is the backstory of so many brands and successful influencers including, Sara Blakely, Founder and CEO of the world-famous Spanx brand. The brand that literally changes women's lives and how they feel daily. In a Business Insider article, she shared how she dealt with rejection and failed a lot before she became the Founder of the

Spanx brand. She recounted all the careers that did not quite make the cut from not making it as a stand-up comedian, or becoming a lawyer because she failed the LSAT twice, or even passing the audition for the Goofy character at Disney because she was too short. She finally found something stable selling fax machines which she did for seven years. But even in that role, she dealt with rejection daily on cold calls. Even after she came up with the Spanx idea she had to deal with double rejection from cold calls during her day job and rejection from North Carolina factories to produce her prototype.

But the only way she was able to become the billionaire Founder of Spanx was not because of her innovative idea, sophisticated business plan, or hosts of investors, but her resiliency to keep going when others said, "No."

You have everything you need to run and sustain a successful company - everything. The most critical thing you can do for yourself and your business is to change your thinking. Successful women think differently. They act differently. And they talk to themselves differently. They tell themselves who they are instead of who they are not. They control their thinking and do not let their thinking control them. Yes, there will be off days, but being fully aware keeps those days as an exception and not the rule.

Listed below are a few **Successful Business Women Affirmations** to start each day and get your focus in the right direction:

- Money comes easy to me
- People are seeking out my specific services
- I am a leader in my industry
- My company is incomparable to others
- I have everything I need to go to the next level
- I am innovative and creative
- Clients and contracts are waiting on me
- I was made for radical success
- Mistakes and failure do not define me
- Wealth is my legacy

Do you have more? Take some time to write out a few more and commit to saying them daily.

# Notes & Reflections

# For Her Progress

Melissa J. Nixon

# 28 GOALS, RESULTS, & REFLECTIONS:

*"You are allowed to be a masterpiece and a work in progress simultaneously." -The Red Fairy Project*

The *Profit Playbook for Women* takes a 360 approach to goal-setting, results, and reflections. Your business results are not just about revenue and profits. It's about the health of *you* and your business which includes you, your team, your family, and friends.

In this section, we will look at your progress including everything from your goals, your results, and your reflections on why you are where you are.

What gets measured, gets DONE!

**When you look at your business, answer the following questions:**

What are you focusing on?

What are you measuring?

What else do you need to measure?

**A business that operates without a target is not a business at all.**

Your business goals should not just be S.M.A.R.T., they should be highly intelligent. This means you are setting specific, measurable, attainable, results-oriented and timely goals based on the following:

- What's happened in your business in the *past*
- What's happening in your *industry*
- What's happening in the *economy*
- What's happening with **your target audience**

We've all heard of S.M.A.R.T. goals but what does that mean for your business?

| | |
|---|---|
| Specific Yet Stretching | Vague goals do nothing for your growth. Is your goal about revenue? Clients? Marketing? Does it have a tangible outcome? |
| Measurable | Goals are great, but what processes and metrics will you have in place to measure your progress? |
| Attainable | Ensure that your goals are within reach. Make sure |

| | |
|---|---|
| | to identify the small wins along the way. |
| Results-Oriented & Relevant | It is easy to set all kinds of goals but they should be relevant to the outcome you are looking for. If your goal is to grow profits, your tasks should all be related to that. |
| Timely | Every goal should have a preset time limit. Beyond stating to achieve X goal in X fiscal year, set smaller quarterly goals that will help break down the larger goal. |

Each industry has different key metrics; However, there are standard metrics every business should be monitoring on a monthly, quarterly and annual basis:

- Revenue
- Expenses
- Profit
- Client Conversion
- Marketing/Brand Awareness
- Client Satisfaction
- Attrition/Turnover
- Other industry-specific metrics

No matter how your business calendar runs, Jan - Dec, July - Jun, etc. you and your team should always have an annual strategic planning meeting or retreat. This is the time set aside to:

- Reflect on where you've been
- Celebrate your accomplishments
- Recalibrate where you said you wanted to go
- Create the plan/roadmap to get there in the months ahead

This annual process then becomes your guide for the entire year helping you to know where to focus each quarter in terms of your time, finances and resources because of the strategic goals you created. There are a number of strategic planning models that are available and they all work. The key is that the process is a part of your business model on an annual basis.

In this section, you will find templates to help you plan, measure and track your results for the entire year, by year, by quarter and month.

# 29 ANNUAL GOALS

**Year:** _____

| Area of Life: | Annual Goals: |
|---|---|
| Business | |
| Personal | |
| Family | |
| Health | |

# Quarterly Goals

# 30 QUARTERLY GOALS

**Quarter:** _____

| Area of Life: | Quarterly Goals: |
|---|---|
| Business | |
| Personal | |
| Family | |
| Health | |

# QUARTERLY RESULTS & REFLECTIONS:

**Quarter:** _____

| Area of Life: | Results & Reflections: |
|---|---|
| Business | |
| Personal | |
| Family | |
| Health | |

# QUARTERLY RESULTS & REFLECTIONS:

**When you look back over the past quarter:**

What are you most proud of?

What would you do differently?

What did you learn?

# QUARTERLY GOALS

**Quarter:** _____

| Area of Life: | Quarterly Goals: |
|---|---|
| Business | |
| Personal | |
| Family | |
| Health | |

# QUARTERLY RESULTS & REFLECTIONS:

**Quarter:** _____

| Area of Life: | Results & Reflections: |
|---|---|
| Business | |
| Personal | |
| Family | |
| Health | |

# QUARTERLY RESULTS & REFLECTIONS:

**When you look back over the past quarter:**

What are you most proud of?

What would you do differently?

What did you learn?

# QUARTERLY GOALS

**Quarter:** _____

| Area of Life: | Quarterly Goals: |
| --- | --- |
| Business | |
| Personal | |
| Family | |
| Health | |

# QUARTERLY RESULTS & REFLECTIONS:

**Quarter:** _____

| Area of Life: | Results & Reflections: |
|---|---|
| Business | |
| Personal | |
| Family | |
| Health | |

# QUARTERLY RESULTS & REFLECTIONS:

**When you look back over the past quarter:**

What are you most proud of?

What would you do differently?

What did you learn?

# QUARTERLY GOALS

**Quarter:** _____

| Area of Life: | Quarterly Goals: |
|---|---|
| Business | |
| Personal | |
| Family | |
| Health | |

# QUARTERLY RESULTS & REFLECTIONS:

**Quarter:** _____

| Area of Life: | Results & Reflections: |
|---|---|
| Business | |
| Personal | |
| Family | |
| Health | |

## QUARTERLY RESULTS & REFLECTIONS:

**When you look back over the past quarter:**

What are you most proud of?

What would you do differently?

What did you learn?

# Monthly
# Goals

# 31 MONTHLY GOALS

**Month:** _____

| Area of Life: | Monthly Goals: |
|---|---|
| Business | |
| Personal | |
| Family | |
| Health | |

# MONTHLY RESULTS & REFLECTIONS:

**Month:** _____

| Area of Life: | Results & Reflections: |
|---|---|
| Business | |
| Personal | |
| Family | |
| Health | |

# MONTHLY GOALS

**Month:** _____

| Area of Life: | Monthly Goals: |
|---|---|
| Business | |
| Personal | |
| Family | |
| Health | |

# MONTHLY RESULTS & REFLECTIONS:

**Month:** _____

| Area of Life: | Results & Reflections: |
|---|---|
| Business | |
| Personal | |
| Family | |
| Health | |

# MONTHLY GOALS

**Month:** _____

| Area of Life: | Monthly Goals: |
|---|---|
| Business | |
| Personal | |
| Family | |
| Health | |

# MONTHLY RESULTS & REFLECTIONS:

**Month:** _____

| Area of Life: | Results & Reflections: |
|---|---|
| Business | |
| Personal | |
| Family | |
| Health | |

# MONTHLY GOALS

**Month:** _____

| Area of Life: | Monthly Goals: |
|---|---|
| Business | |
| Personal | |
| Family | |
| Health | |

# MONTHLY RESULTS & REFLECTIONS:

**Month:** _____

| Area of Life: | Results & Reflections: |
|---|---|
| Business | |
| Personal | |
| Family | |
| Health | |

# MONTHLY GOALS

**Month:** _____

| Area of Life: | Monthly Goals: |
|---|---|
| Business | |
| Personal | |
| Family | |
| Health | |

# MONTHLY RESULTS & REFLECTIONS:

**Month:** _____

| Area of Life: | Results & Reflections: |
|---|---|
| Business | |
| Personal | |
| Family | |
| Health | |

# MONTHLY GOALS

**Month:** _____

| Area of Life: | Monthly Goals: |
|---|---|
| Business | |
| Personal | |
| Family | |
| Health | |

# MONTHLY RESULTS & REFLECTIONS:

**Month:** _____

| Area of Life: | Results & Reflections: |
|---|---|
| Business | |
| Personal | |
| Family | |
| Health | |

# MONTHLY GOALS

**Month:** _____

| Area of Life: | Monthly Goals: |
|---|---|
| Business | |
| Personal | |
| Family | |
| Health | |

# MONTHLY RESULTS & REFLECTIONS:

**Month:** _____

| Area of Life: | Results & Reflections: |
|---|---|
| Business | |
| Personal | |
| Family | |
| Health | |

# MONTHLY GOALS

**Month:** _____

| Area of Life: | Monthly Goals: |
|---|---|
| Business | |
| Personal | |
| Family | |
| Health | |

# MONTHLY RESULTS & REFLECTIONS:

**Month:** _____

| Area of Life: | Results & Reflections: |
|---|---|
| Business | |
| Personal | |
| Family | |
| Health | |

# MONTHLY GOALS

**Month:** _____

| Area of Life: | Monthly Goals: |
|---|---|
| Business | |
| Personal | |
| Family | |
| Health | |

# MONTHLY RESULTS & REFLECTIONS:

**Month:** _____

| Area of Life: | Results & Reflections: |
|---|---|
| Business | |
| Personal | |
| Family | |
| Health | |

# MONTHLY GOALS

**Month:** _____

| Area of Life: | Monthly Goals: |
|---|---|
| Business | |
| Personal | |
| Family | |
| Health | |

# MONTHLY RESULTS & REFLECTIONS:

**Month:** _____

| Area of Life: | Results & Reflections: |
|---|---|
| Business | |
| Personal | |
| Family | |
| Health | |

# MONTHLY GOALS

**Month:** _____

| Area of Life: | Monthly Goals: |
|---|---|
| Business | |
| Personal | |
| Family | |
| Health | |

# MONTHLY RESULTS & REFLECTIONS:

**Month:** _____

| Area of Life: | Results & Reflections: |
|---|---|
| Business | |
| Personal | |
| Family | |
| Health | |

# MONTHLY GOALS

**Month:** _____

| Area of Life: | Monthly Goals: |
|---|---|
| Business | |
| Personal | |
| Family | |
| Health | |

# MONTHLY RESULTS & REFLECTIONS:

**Month:** _____

| Area of Life: | Results & Reflections: |
|---|---|
| Business | |
| Personal | |
| Family | |
| Health | |

# A Year in Review

# 32 A YEAR IN REVIEW

| Area of Life: | A Year in Review: |
|---|---|
| Business | |
| Personal | |
| Family | |
| Health | |

# A YEAR IN REVIEW

**When you look back on the past year:**

What are you most proud of?

What would you do differently?

What did you learn?

# Notes & Reflections

_____

_____

_____

_____

_____

_____

_____

_____

_____

_____

_____

_____

_____

_____

_____

_____

_____

_____

_____

_____

_____

_____

_____

_____

# ABOUT THE AUTHOR

Melissa Nixon is a sought-after business and leadership development consultant, speaker, and trainer. She is the Founder of the Courageous Life Academy a leadership and business development consulting firm and the author of, The Courageous Life - How to Leap from Your Career to Your Calling. She prepares, positions, and pushes leaders, individuals and organizations to make their next courageous move. Melissa is known for the success of her program development for organizations such as CVMSDC and the Women's Business Center of Charlotte. As a result, she was awarded the Presidential Award for her work in leadership and small business development from the Carolinas Virginia Minority Supplier Development Council.

This executive coach and captivating keynote speaker is known for being a thought-driver to leaders and audiences nationally and internationally. Melissa's motto is "I'm not afraid of failure, I'm afraid of regret." Her desire is the same for other leaders and organizations. As a result, she pushes them both to lead courageously!

### *Melissa's Motto* is,

*"I'm not afraid of failure but I am afraid of regret!"*

*Invite Melissa to coach, speak or train*
*at your organization*
*Hello@courageouslifeacademy.com*

www.ingramcontent.com/pod-product-compliance
Lightning Source LLC
Chambersburg PA
CBHW050121210326
41519CB00015BA/4050